# THE POWER OF HABIT

*How to achieve nothing in life or create atomic habits of success*

**KATHERINE CURTIS**

# TABLE OF CONTENTS

INTRODUCTION ...................................................................................1

**CHAPTER 1**..................................................................................**3**
WHAT ARE HABITS?

    The Habit Loop ...........................................................................5

**CHAPTER 2** ...............................................................................**6**
HOW HABITS FORM

**CHAPTER 3** ...............................................................................**8**
THE POWER OF HABITS.................................................................8

**CHAPTER 4** ..............................................................................**11**
HOW BAD HABITS CAN RUIN YOU

    Affect Relationships ................................................................ 12

    Impact on Finances ................................................................ 13

    Make You Lose Opportunities................................................ 15

    Health Issues........................................................................... 15

    Stall Growth in Life................................................................ 17

**CHAPTER 5** .............................................................................**18**
NEGATIVE HABITS TO CUT OUT

    Procrastination......................................................................... 19

    Poor Time Management .......................................................... 19

    Smoking and Excessive Drinking............................................ 20

    Excessive Gambling................................................................. 20

Poor Hygiene ........................................................................... 21

Impulsive Buying and Excessive Online Shopping ............................ 21

Swearing .............................................................................. 21

Social Media Addiction .............................................................. 22

## CHAPTER 6 ..............................................................................23
ESSENTIAL TIPS FOR BREAKING NEGATIVE HABITS

Identify, understand, and research your habit ........................... 24

Avoid triggers ....................................................................... 24

Make a commitment, and use your motivation wave ........................ 25

Make a plan ......................................................................... 25

Get help .............................................................................. 25

Build a network of support ...................................................... 26

Set milestones ...................................................................... 26

Swap habits .......................................................................... 26

Quitting cold turkey? .............................................................. 27

## CHAPTER 7 ..............................................................................28
WHY YOU NEED GOOD PRODUCTIVE HABITS

Be Able to Persevere Better ...................................................... 29

Build Healthier Working Relationships ....................................... 29

Stand Out ............................................................................ 30

Supercharge Your Way to Success .............................................. 30

## CHAPTER 8 ..............................................................................31
POSITIVE HABITS YOU SHOULD IMBIBE

Wake up Early ....................................................................... 32

Meditate .............................................................................. 32

Exercising ............................................................................ 32

Eating Healthy............................................................................ 33

Read and Write........................................................................... 33

Set Goals.................................................................................... 33

Perseverance............................................................................... 34

Positive Thinking........................................................................ 34

Develop Money Management Skills.............................................. 34

Cultivate Social Skills.................................................................. 35

CONCLUSION ............................................................................. 36

# INTRODUCTION

In life, we all want the same things first and foremost, happiness and success. That is the basis of our everyday struggle and sacrifice. Everyone wants to be successful at work and in school. We all want to have a happy professional life and a loving, caring family behind us. Everyone wants their aims to be fulfilled after they have put in the prerequisite effort needed. Nobody wants to fail or get to experience failure in their attempts to succeed. Yet, sadly, more people get to fail than those who succeed. Most people experience happiness once in a while, but the frequency is much lower than what they would want ordinarily and ideally. Therefore, for every success in the business world, there are a thousand failures. For every person at his dream job, there are a million people out there slaving and working away at the last place they would rather be working.

So, what is the difference between the super-successful and happy people of this world and every other average individual out there on the streets? What do the Steve Jobs, Einsteins, Trumps, Beyonces, Picassos and Bezos have in spades that every other Tom, Dick, and Harry on the street seem to lack? HABITS!!! They have abundant good, productive habits that favor what they were trying to achieve. As Brian Tracy said; "Successful people are simply those with successful habits."

We are who our habits say we are. Our habits not only guide us and make things simpler for us; they actually draw our character and path through life. It is basic and really simple. Build up negative habits that impede your goals, and you can be sure you will never get there. On the other hand, if you spare the right kind of effort and enough time to foster the right habits to help you maximize your potential, the effects will be astounding, to say the least.

Your habits are the singularly most powerful predictor of just how well or how badly you are going to perform at a task or thing. Do you want to succeed and live a happy life? You need to create the habits that will facilitate that for you. It doesn't matter if you are a teenager, adult, or in your late sixties. This rule always applies without exception. Do you want to avoid persistent stress and failure? Then, you need to destroy the negative habits that can hold you back.

This brings us to the whole point of this book. A lot of people already know that our habits play such a pivotal role in our lives yet only a few actually realize that we have the power to choose our habits. Most people seem to develop habits subconsciously. They find something they like doing, and it automatically becomes a part of them. They do not know how to get rid of it even when it is clear that it is harming them in a big way. I wrote this book precisely to get you out of that fix if you are in it.

If our habits are going to determine our lives, then it becomes imperative on us to get rid of the not-too-good ones and replace them with more positive habits that are sure to boost our chances of achieving our aims. The means of doing both is contained within this book. You only need to commit to putting the knowledge you pick up here to practice. A word of caution: breaking old habits is one of the most difficult mental acts a man can do. However, if you put in the right kind of mental effort, you can learn to choose only the beneficial habits you actually need in life and discard the rest.

Good luck!!!

# CHAPTER 1
# WHAT ARE HABITS?

*"Our character is basically a composite of our habits. Because they are consistent, often unconscious patterns, they constantly, daily, express our character."*

—Stephen Covey

The human brain is quite a complex biological structure, perhaps the most complex one on Planet Earth. It is able to perform unbelievably intricate permutations and handle large tasks simultaneously. However, even the human brain has limits beyond which it performs at a suboptimal level. There are far too many things for the brain to do than devote its resources to repeating the same acts in full-blown conscious mode. This gave rise to habits.

Remember those little shortcuts on your computer desktop, the ones that shorten the effort and time you need to complete tasks or navigate your own personal computers? Well, habits are like the mental version of those shortcuts. They are the brain's way of maximizing its own power.

Do you remember learning how to drive? How you had to pay full attention each time you shifted gears? Initially, because it was something new and novel to you, you probably needed to pay conscious attention to changing the gears. However, as you got better and repeated the same act, your brain simply stored the sequence of events you need it to perform each time you want to change gears and initiate this sequence each time.

That is exactly how each one of your habits developed. When you repeat something often enough, your brain starts to classify it as a habit, something it can develop well enough that you wouldn't need full consciousness to activate. In pretty much the same way you would click a desktop shortcut, your brain simply waits for you to give the command and you can execute that habit on an almost subconscious level once the trigger is right.

Now, when you look around your life well, you will realize that quite a lot of what we do every day is down to habit. Humans are creatures of routine, and our routine is nothing but a collection of habits. The most recent scientific studies seem to agree with Jack D. Hodge's statement that "Habits are important. Up to 90 percent of our everyday behavior is based on habit. Nearly all of what we do each day, every day, is simply a habit."

The way we walk, talk, eat, dress, and interact with one another is mostly down to the habits we have formed. Therefore, our uniqueness as separate individuals also has a lot to do with the fact that we all have a different set of habits that define us.

# The Habit Loop

After we have formed them, we repeat habits in three phases and based on the presence of three variables; the trigger, routine, and reward. For you to act out a habit, you need a trigger to tell your brain to set the ball rolling. Getting up from bed may trigger your morning routine made of habits such as brushing your teeth, taking a bath, and dressing up. The presence of a very complex task before you may cause you to engage your procrastination habit. You get the idea, right?

The next thing is the routine, the habit itself. When the trigger is present, then your brain carries out the habit itself. That could be brushing, eating, or any other of the thousand habits we all have. This phase is carried out almost always subconsciously. You get to eat without focusing on how to lift your spoon or chew food for instance. Instead, you do all these automatically.

Why do we keep repeating habits though? It is because the last stage provides some form of reward for us. It could be feeling high after smoking or the safety of knowing that by taking your bath regularly, you are keeping clean. Each habit provides us with some form of reward, real or imagined, that ensures that we repeat it once the trigger is present.

# CHAPTER 2
# HOW HABITS FORM

*"The chains of habit are too weak to be felt until they are too strong to be broken."*

—*Samuel Johnson*

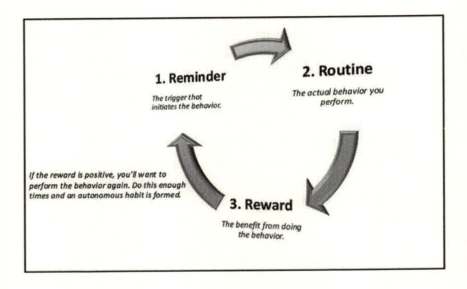

Habit formation has been a hot topic in psychology and neuroscience for some time. There are still some gray areas in our understanding of the issue even now. However, it has been proven that the striatum, a part of the basal ganglia in the human brain is responsible for habit formation and execution. When we consciously act, the prefrontal cortex in the brain is often responsible for that, but with time, repeated acts become habits that the brain stores in the basal ganglia.

What happens is that each time you add a new act to your routine, it burns a neural path in the brain. It is like a river branching out in a new direction; it continues to weave and widen its new path. So, each time you repeat the act, the path it has created in your brain gets deeper and "more permanent." It is a bit like wearing out a new footpath on grass; the more people that tread the new path, the clearer it becomes. When you have repeated the habit well enough, it becomes very easy for your brain to carry it out at the semi-conscious level that characterizes habit, as it now has an easy path to follow.

Habits, especially negative ones, may also form under the influence of certain hormones in the body. Why do you think people smoke even though the cigarettes they smoke carry a warning against smoking? It is simply because each time we carry out an act that gives us thrills such as our favorite sport or certain destructive habit, two hormones serotonin and dopamine, responsible for happiness and a feeling of elation are released. They are responsible for the feelings of being high that drug abusers receive and that sardonic pleasure one might get off chewing one's nails.

Now, as humans, we have different thresholds of tolerance. Some people get a feel of this delight and are able to resist turning the act that produced it into a habit, especially if it's a negative one. Others are less able to resist and become kind of addicted to the hormonal rush of adrenaline that they get from negative acts. That can foster the production and permanence of such habits if kept up.

Whatever the case, whatever you repeatedly do soon carves out a space for itself in your brain so to speak. Habits develop as time and effort-saving acts but may also arise from an addiction to hormonal thrills and kicks.

# CHAPTER 3
# THE POWER OF HABITS

*"We first make our habits, and then our habits make us."*

—John Dryden

It is simple to see really. Our fate is decided by our actions; habits represent our favorite actions. So, we are what our habits are. There is barely any task that we do that doesn't incorporate a bit of the habit logic. Our brain would be overloaded otherwise. Let us look at the different classes of habits.

Broadly, there are three main classes of habits. The first class comprises of the day-to-day habits that keep our lives running smoothly such as taking our bath, driving, eating, and going to work. They are not harmful and are important for us to get along well. The second class of habits is positive habits. Granted, they often require a bit more effort than the first class but then, they provide you great benefits when kept up for some time. Such habits may include being punctual in school always, reading wide to accrue knowledge or having a functional saving and money-management plan. The last class of habits is negative habits, which are destructive, harmful, and self-limiting habits that slow down our progress. These are the ones we must work upon to limit their impacts.

In their own way, every single one of these habits is powerful and has the power to shape our lives, for good or for bad. Forget the opportunities you are going to get for a moment; they aren't as important as what you do with them, and what you do with them is going to be determined by your habits. If you have good habits, you will find it easier to turn your opportunities into success. If you have negative habits like delaying your actions, you will find it extra hard to turn these opportunities into gold.

Even the obstacles and setbacks we all are going to face aren't nearly as important as the way we approach them. Some people are quitters; others are battlers who face their troubles and dispel them. Which of these groups is more likely to overcome any setback they face? Your habits are that powerful. They determine what sort of individual and character profile you are going to have. They have the final say on what you should be called; a happy man, an angry individual, a success, a chronic failure, a quitter or an achiever? We simply cannot become anything aside from our habits. The average sum of your habits is going to represent you, in your absence and presence. They are going to determine the way you talk, walk, read, do business, or communicate with people.

Bill Gates is famous the world over for his habit of smiling at all times. That has helped him, aside from his wealth, to cultivate an image of a confident, assured entrepreneur. Cristiano Ronaldo, the superstar footballer, was talented at an early age but many more talented young footballers have failed to arrive at superstardom. How did he make it?

Teammates and coaches have attributed his success to his ability of constantly practicing more than anybody else. Day after day, he practiced and practiced until he was the best he could be. Jack Dorsey, the co-founder of Twitter, wakes up early at 5:30 am each day, meditates for thirty minutes, and follows that up with a six-mile jog. That leaves him feeling fit, fresh, and energized by the time he needs to make business and work decisions. Such is the power of habits. Almost every successful person has his own unique set of conscious, developed habits that have aided their rise to the top.

Very importantly too, most habits last for long. For instance, if you write off your neighbor on a desk at school, the chances are higher that you will eventually grow up illiterate and bitter, and you will not be able to have a decent income. If you make smoking a habit, you can expect to fall sick due to the smoke later on in life and probably have very poor health as a result of this habit. If you possess a chronic gambling habit, financial stability will be far from you. If on the other hand, you take each night to plan the next day, you are bound to have smoother, well-coordinated days. If you read well and wide, you will be better informed and enlightened than someone who spends most of their time in front of a television watching soap operas.

The almost permanent nature of habits makes it almost impossible to discontinue them. A vast majority of the habits you have today were picked up from a much younger age. Think back to your high school days and the friends you kept. Now, look at those friends you still have around from then, and you will find out that they all still retain vestiges of their character and habits from back then. The guy who always studied hard then may still be that same suave, composed, and thoughtful friend today.

Therefore, dear reader, if you are young, you need to work out habits that will make your life better in the long run. If you are an adult, it is time to look around your formed habits and decide which ones are positive and should be kept and which are negative that should be replaced.

# CHAPTER 4
# HOW BAD HABITS CAN RUIN YOU

*"Depending on what they are, our habits will either make us or break us. We become what we repeatedly do."*

—*Sean Covey*

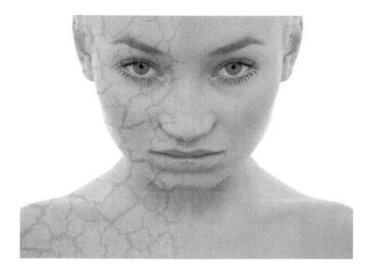

Habits are vehicles invented by man himself to bring his eventual success or ruin. While I will ask you to pardon my use of the words 'man' and 'his' as is the convention to do so when referring to the humankind, I am not sorry for the assertion that habits lead to eventual ruin or success. Why? It is a fact that has been repeatedly demonstrated in life. You will see it around if not within you. Yes, we are creatures of habits, but that does not mean which should let ourselves be possessed or taken over by the kind of habits that cause our regression rather than progress.

Perhaps you do not believe that habits, bad habits specifically, can ruin the chances of your success. Perhaps you just doubt how a simple act of biting your nails can cost you so much, or how being online on Facebook or Instagram for a good part of your day can lead to lowered levels of productivity. If you have these and other doubts, then allow me the privilege to convince you that some of those little acts you take for granted go a long way to affect your life. In this chapter, I shall make attempts to break down the illusions which bad habits have deftly set up to blind us to their real nature, the real effects on our lives.

I must tell you that the list of the harmful effects of bad habits on our lives can be inexhaustive, as you will figure out soon. However, in this chapter, I have for the sake of brevity and precision limited myself to explaining only a handful of such effects. The ones I shall explain, I believe, will have encompassed some others which you may likely think up while reading the next couple of chapters.

## Affect Relationships

Whether it started on one cold winter evening at a bar when you had a bet you could finish twenty glasses of beer and still remain perfectly sober, or whether it started on one warm summer afternoon at the park when an ad popped up on your phone advertising a new video game that has been gaining so many positive ratings lately, one fact remains: whichever way it must have started, whichever way you must have picked them up, bad habits affect your relationships. Even stranger, it does not affect only one of the many types of relationship there are; it affects all types of relationship, social and professional.

How bad habits affect your relationships and the types of relationship they affect depends on the bad habit in question. Some people have made a habit of promising things they know with a certainty they will not do. They go around giving assurances and putting people's minds at ease that once they have given their word, they won't break it. Yet, such persons are wont to do the very thing they say and make people believe they will not do. They break their word as the sun breaks every morning with a consistency that seldom breaks. Others will certainly start seeing such persons as liars and develop a kind of mistrust for them. Even their closest associates doubt them and find it difficult to vouch for them.

Worse even, the mistrust will not be limited to when they give their words alone, it will extend to other things. Entrusting such persons with delicate matters or positions of trust becomes extremely difficult. If such a person is a professional, his relationship with his colleagues who want to confer with him get strained and so do his relationships with his clients.

Allow me to use another habit, alcoholism, as an example. If this is the bad habit you have formed, your case is perhaps even much worse. Habitual excessive drinking gradually distances you from your family first. You may have a wife who is ashamed of you, who regrets she has chosen you. You will have a wife who is terrified the kids might take after you. You will have kids who cannot look up to you for emulation. In such situations, mothers, being the caring creatures they are, will instantly choose the children over you, and in so doing, will rather prefer to break ties with you, taking the kids away from you. And no court will certainly allow you to have custody of such children, not when your excessive drinking is the ground for the divorce. I can choose another bad habit and bring up illustrations on how it can affect your relationships with others. I can show you how spending so much time on video games can cost you the best of moments with your little daughter who wants to play with you. However, I believe you understand better at this point.

## Impact on Finances

Most bad habits can impact negatively on your finances. This they can do directly or indirectly in small incremental steps until the loss becomes too big for you to gloss over. The world is hard enough with enough money to cover your needs. When you do not have enough on account of a destructive habit, then one can say you are on a suicidal mission. You need money to pay for products, the newspaper subscription, milk, foodstuff, etc. You need money to pay for services such as a new painting job for your porch, water, and electricity bills, etc. That money may come easily to you, or you may belong to the group who have to toil day and night to earn it. Whichever of these you belong to, you are not immune from ruining your finances owing to bad habits.

It could be the little change you paid for booze on a night after work. It could be the few coins you inserted into the slot machine on the weekend at the casino. Remember, all it takes to set the fiery ball of financial damnation rolling is to make a habit of these acts. Imagine someone who experiments with online gambling for the very first time – it is sweet because he is able to make a few bucks off it then perhaps the algorithm notices a newcomer it needs to retain. Then you go back to the website to make some more easy money. Then you go the next day, and this continues until you start racking up credit card debts.

The above may sound too obvious as a bad habit. Let me tell you about another subtle one that ruins your finances. This other one is harmless; it prays on the thrill to own and the excitement to show off what we own. It is a simple act of acquiring an excessive interest in material possessions. This is an act that has been made easy when everything came online. I am talking of an insatiable desire to shop and buy things you don't really need. You only need to see the stats. This act has become a bad habit that has ruined the lives of many people. Worse still, you may be bestowing that habit to your child who watches as you flip through ads and click the "add to cart button" and pay later. Before you know it, you will have racked up too much debt that your means of living cannot support. For this, you need to break the bad habits that eat into your finances and enjoy the peace of living without the specter of debts looming large over you.

## Make You Lose Opportunities

As I stated at the beginning of this chapter, different bad habits have different negative effects on your life. Opportunities are important in life; they may come as a right or as a privilege. When an opportunity comes as a right, say a promotion at work, it also comes with conditions attached. You may be required to be the one with perfect punctuality before you can be considered for the position. But here you are, with the perfect profile for the job except for one chink in your professional armor; you are notorious for being a latecomer. How can you be considered for the position? How can a company risk you go late to an important investment meeting or any meeting at all?

Your bad habit may be procrastination. What is wrong with stalling the completion of a job for a few more days when you have a month to complete it? One thing, just one thing is wrong; when that day comes, you push it forward again. This continues until the panic monkey within you wakes up to the reality of the deadline. Then you will realize the few days left are not enough to complete the job.

You ask for an extension, and it is not granted. The D-day comes, and you are unable to deliver. Your client cancels the job, for example, after you send them a piece of it to show your progress. Not only have you lost the job, but also lose future opportunities with the same client. And since clients talk, word spreads around of your professional competence. Disappoint two clients and your rating in the business community takes a fall. It is even worse when you have built a great reputation for yourself. I can go on and on with several other examples and illustrations. Yet, they will all only serve to hammer it in that bad habits can wreck the opportunities you have to succeed.

## Health Issues

I am sure the few examples and illustrations given so far are enough to help you vividly picture how bad habits can impact negatively on your health. Take a bad habit as simple as nail-biting. The clearing and forwarding process you perform on that part of your body has the potential to make you sick to the bone. There are dirt and germs around. From the door of the toilet through the balustrade in your office building to the many handshakes you receive a day, you have a great many opportunities to pick up germs with your hands. Yet, it is the same hand that you irresistibly take to your mouth all the time, mowing the outgrowth of the thin horny coverings that grow on the upper surface of the end of your fingers with your teeth. Saying it in so many words downplays the effect, maybe. In simple terms, biting your teeth poses a dangerous if not the existential threat to your life.

Other bad habits such as overeating too could pose real threats to your health. If you are the type that cannot resist the urge of constantly feeling something go down your throat, then obesity is quite close to you. It is easier to gain weight than to lose it. Adding a few extra pounds here and there may seem harmless at first, but when the effects of having too much mass set in, you may start hating yourself and those friends who were not kind enough to point out your excessive eating was coming to this end.

I do not even need to demystify how smoking kills you gradually. It is not just some clichéd expression when they say smokers are liable to die young. Smoking kills, that's the golden truth. But there are more dimensions to health than just physical health. What about mental or psychological health? How do bad habits impair this? The answer is: in a lot of ways.

Take an uncontrollable urge to use social media. If you are the type that has become glued to the popular social networks because of the Likes and Thumbs up you get when you upload your pictures and short videos of your life, when you don't get the admiration expressed by some others with the tap of a button on their screen, a little sadness may be the next thing you feel. But before you know what's happening, depression might be just around the corner, waiting patiently to pounce on you. Why? Because you made yourself dependent on social media. Bad habits can therefore easily ruin one's health, physical and mental.

## Stall Growth in Life

You may have any one or more of the many bad habits there are. If you do, then you are also very much susceptible to more than one of the effects of bad habits there are. When you start combining the negative effects of bad habits in your life, the chain of reaction can be literally ruining. Imagine not being able to pay the premiums on your health insurance because you virtually owe too much. What happens when lung cancer due to constant smoking is not discovered early enough? If you are pinned down by health problems such as this or some other, your productivity dips as you are unable to get a job or you lose your job from becoming a liability.

The simple implication of this is that when you allow yourself to be conquered by one bad habit, it may throw you into a cycle of misfortune from which you may not recover in life. Remember, the list of bad habits is almost inexhaustive. From constantly making in-app purchases to unlock the next level of a game you constantly play on your phone, to wearing the same underwear over and over again without washing, you invite more than you can cope with into your life. And when they come, it may be too late to turn back the hand of the clock.

To grow, one must have the right set of habits to foment rapid personal self-development. If instead, you possess too many negative habits, your growth will be stunted, and progress will be harder than it necessarily needs to be.

# CHAPTER 5
# NEGATIVE HABITS TO CUT OUT

*"It is easier to prevent bad habits than to break them."*

—*Benjamin Franklin*

Previously in this book, I have explained what habits are and how they form. In this chapter, the aim is to bring you closer to the nature and world of bad habits by discussing some prominent bad habits. These are things you probably know or have heard of. There are those you would probably not even suspect to be bad habits. The selection in this chapter is not random. I should add. I have singled out the habits discussed because they relate to success and failure in life. The habits discussed here are to be avoided in order to steer clear of failure and achieve success in life. What else are we waiting for? Let us get to know the uncanny acts that can become a cog in the wheel of your progress in life if allowed to flourish.

# Procrastination

What is procrastination? I will rather not bore you with some technical or dictionary definitions. Allow me to tell you simply what procrastination is by way of illustration. We say you procrastinate when you have formed a habit of leaving a pressing task undone for another less important task. There is nothing wrong with leaving a task to do it later, but it must be for the right reasons. If you are fond of delaying action for no compelling or tenable reason, then you are a procrastinator, and you need to work to stamp it out of your life.

One negative effect of procrastination on your life is that it can cost you opportunities. You may think you have more than a month to start applying for that scholarship. So, rather than starting the application process now, you leave it for later. When a week to the deadline you start the application process, you may realize that the reference letters from your referees have to be submitted before the deadline, too. Thus, despite having met all other requirements for the scholarship, not getting your application done within the stipulated time because of procrastination means you have denied yourself the opportunity to get the scholarship. Procrastination is the thief of time quite alright, but it also steals success away from you.

# Poor Time Management

Do not confuse poor time management with procrastination. Yes, there may be some overlap because procrastination is mismanagement of the time you have to get a task done. Yet, they differ because general time management is a much broader topic that deals with how you use your time. If you combine both the bad habit of procrastination and poor time management, you may have hit the best recipe for failure. You need to break free from the cycle of poor time management.

In life, you need to understand that everyone has the same amount of time, 24 hours a day. You also need to realize that others may buy themselves more time by buying into yours. Your employer needs more time on his hand for some other things and thus pays you to spend yours on a job which he benefits from. Yet, two things are involved: one, you should not spend all your time building someone else's dream; and two, you cannot waste time on the job for the sake of efficiency. Because of these two, you should know you must never waste time. You can do this by cultivating the good habit of maximizing the time you have and using it judiciously. Losing track of time is a bad habit that can produce harmful effects. You need to learn to schedule your day, assign time periods to everything you have to do, and follow your plan unless it is necessary you deviate.

## Smoking and Excessive Drinking

Smoking and excessive drinking are two bad habits that often coexist in the same individual. Yet you may very well have one and not the other. Smoking may involve cigarettes or some other substances such as marijuana. If you are sufficiently familiar with the harmful effects of these on your health, you will certainly realize every suck on the roll brings you a step closer to suffering and discomfort in life. You may have invested time in some worthy enterprise but adding smoking to the list of your habits may well rob you of the opportunity to reap the fruits of your labor.

In the same vein, excessive drinking is a bad habit that many fall victims. It starts with an innocent taste of alcohol probably before you even come of age or upon your eighteenth birthday. But what started as an innocent act may progress into a habit that will later cost you in life in terms of finances, relationships, and even health. A chronic drunk is a social embarrassment to his family and himself. It is one habit you can do without.

## Excessive Gambling

Gambling can be an enjoyable leisure activity if proper management and personal rules are applied. As long as you keep it safe, it can be quite a refreshing experience. The moment you lose control over the amount of gambling you do and the attendant losses that it comes with, then there is a big problem. Gambling can ruin your finances and turn you into a liar in no time at all if you want to hide the traces of the habit.

## Poor Hygiene

"Cleanliness is next to godliness," says the adage and for a good reason too. Poor hygiene as a habit can manifest itself in various ways. It can be poor personal hygiene when you are careless about what you wear and your body in general. It can manifest in various ways, such as not brushing your teeth or taking a bath regularly. It could be you not doing your laundry for days on end or living in a scattered, cluttered, dirty living space. If poor hygiene doesn't cost you the best part of your health, it will at least cost you self-confidence when you need it most. Of course, it will also cause you social embarrassment and awkwardness too. It is best stamped out fast.

## Impulsive Buying and Excessive Online Shopping

There is nothing wrong with shopping and buying things, online or offline, at your convenience. What is wrong, however, is not being able to control how much you do this. You should learn to distinguish your needs from your wants; fulfilling the former is essential while the latter is not. Impulsive buying and online shopping eat into your finances until they start to harm you. They also set you on a psychological edge and make you an easy target for soft ads.

## Swearing

Are you one of those who cannot say three words without punctuating them with the F-word? Does the word 'shit' come to your mouth as easily as the stream of breath leave your throat? If these and other swear words come easily to you, you need to change for the better. Saying the "F-word" may not appear harmful until it causes you public disgrace at a formal gathering. The stigma it may generate may not cost you a job or client, but you really do not want to develop a habit that will eventually mark you in negative colors in civilized settings. Do not be the employee the business is afraid to send to a social gathering for fear you may bring them disgrace. It may seem like the in-thing especially for teenagers and young adults, but believe me, you are best off not adding swearing to your habits.

## Social Media Addiction

I have saved this for the last. It is the latest bad habit in vogue. It has spread like a plague, not only amongst the young generations but even amongst the old. The attraction is the attention social media gives us, the increasing figure beside the Facebook Like button or the number of times your tweet has been retweeted. The attraction depends on the platform, and it seems every one of them is designed to keep you hooked. The first way out of this is to realize it can be a bad habit. Excessive attachment to any social media platform can cost your real offline relationships. It may affect your physical communication skills and may even impair your health due to excessive straining of your eyes and craning of your neck.

The negative habits above are just some of the most common. I believe you know even more. Whatever the case, you must work to stamp as many of them as possible out.

# CHAPTER 6
# ESSENTIAL TIPS FOR BREAKING NEGATIVE HABITS

*"Good habits are the key to all success. Bad habits are the unlocked door to failure."*

— *Og Mandino*

In previous chapters, we have discussed how negative habits can damage one's prospects of getting success and happiness in life. I have tried to make you realize why you need to break the yoke that negative habits have upon you. However, breaking negative habits isn't a piece of cake. When you consider the fact that they have burnt a neural tract in our brains, the scope of the task before us truly manifests.

No one can truly be free of negative habits actually, but at the very least, you can attempt to minimize their number and presence. Nevertheless, here are a few tips that can help you fight off any negative habit you are trying to get rid of.

# Identify, understand, and research your habit

Each habit recurs in a distinct pattern. It follows a particular sequence and needs certain prompts before it occurs. "To know thine enemy" is the first commandment of getting rid of negative habits. Realizing you have a particular habit that needs to be changed is essential in getting rid of the habit. Therefore, look at your routine critically. What particular habit do you repeat that you can do away with to boost your productivity? What habit is compromising your health? What habit have the people closest to you complained about? What are the things you regularly do that you are uncomfortable with people getting to know about? Once you have identified such a habit, then you need to read up and research a bit about the habit. You will find other people dealing with the same habit and get good insight on how to win the battle against it.

# Avoid triggers

As I explained under the habit loop, each habit takes three phases to occur. Of these, the easiest one to deal with is the trigger. Triggers come in different forms; the only constant thing is that it is harder to fight off the habit when the trigger is active or present. It could be a group of friends who serve as drinking buddies, email alerts, or loneliness that is the trigger for your bad habits. Going to bed late may be the reason you wake up late for the day's work.

It is going to be a lot easier to fight your alcoholism if you give your drinking buddies some space, and turning off the alerts on your phone will limit the number of times you are urged to check your phone. In the same way, getting to bed earlier will probably make it easier for you to get up early enough in the mornings. Some habits even exist as triggers for other bad habits. Alcoholism or excessive clubbing could precipitate a smoking habit for instance. Whatever the trigger is, just get it far away from you.

Out of sight is not completely out of mind, but it is a good start. Do away with the triggers; they do you no favor.

## Make a commitment, and use your motivation wave

What is the motivation wave? You have a motivation wave right now. At times, we get fired up and all set to take action about something. At times like that, we have the commitment and motivation actually to start acting. However, after some time, we are off the commitment wave, and our desire and ability to act wanes drastically. That is why one can get all fired up and swear not to repeat a particular habit again yet find himself breaking such resolutions only a few days later. How can you prevent this?

Well, you can by using your motivation wave to start something and not just talk about acting. Do not just read this book, get all fired up, and forget everything for instance. Instead, set the ball rolling. See the next point for better insight.

## Make a plan

"He who fails to plan plans to fail" is a common enough saying that needs no explanation. At the very least, use your motivation wave to make a plan for getting rid of an unwanted habit. Habits are hard enough to shoo away with a proper plan. Having no plan or a strong enough reason renders it impossible to see the back of your negative habits. Make it a challenge, do a SWOT analysis, and set up milestones for getting a habit out of your system.

## Get help

Some habits bordering on addictions such as gambling, drug abuse, or smoking may need external or even medical advice. You will do well to get out there and get the help you need. If you ever get the inkling that you may not be able to fight off a particular habit all by yourself, do not be shy about getting external help. Some habits disappear just upon the threat of exposure.

## Build a network of support

Family members and friends are key allies in any psychological or mental struggle, and getting rid of a habit is one big struggle. Having the closest people to you in your corner may make all the difference especially when it comes to monitoring and evaluating your progress. They can help you get back on track when you deviate from your set plan too.

## Set milestones

Set milestones in your plan and reward yourself for reaching them. For instance, if you take too much table sugar and you are trying to cut down, you could draw a plan that has you reducing your intake gradually perhaps by a spoonful per day. When you get to a significant milestone such as going the whole day without sugar, you could buy yourself a new pair of shoes or visit the spa as a reward. By attaching a reward to the milestone, you are rewiring your dopamine rush to favor the annihilation of the negative habit. The brain can be tricked with rewards that turn it against any negative habit.

## Swap habits

However, because our habits are already ingrained in the brain, it is sometimes much easier to swap them for positive habits rather than weed them out entirely. Therefore, you can keep a trigger but just ensure that you have an alternative habit to turn towards when it is in effect. For instance, as a teenager, instead of seeing movies all day, you can pick up a reading habit to swap with your movies. If you grow to like books a lot, you would then just start to reduce the time you spend on movies and spend it on books instead.

## Quitting cold turkey?

Abruptly deciding to stop a habit works for some people. They simply decide to stop a habit and that's all, but this kind of willpower is rare. Therefore, I do not advise you to quit cold-turkey. Instead, focus on small steps that still lead to the same conclusion. Quitting abruptly can make it likelier for you to suffer a relapse simply because the adjustment you need your brain to make was too large. So, take things easy and slow; steady does it.

Getting rid of negative habits isn't a very easy task, but if you can apply these tips, it becomes likelier to happen.

# CHAPTER 7
# WHY YOU NEED GOOD PRODUCTIVE HABITS

*"You'll never change your life until you change something you do daily. The secret of your success is found in your daily routine."*

—John C. Maxwell

Nothing great has ever been achieved without enthusiasm goes a popular saying. I believe with very strong conviction that what is meant by enthusiasm here goes beyond mere passion. It is not enough for you to be passionate about something. You need to take conscious and right steps towards achieving that thing. But what about those who do in fact take conscious, active steps onwards achieving their goals? What else can they do to ensure the steps they are taking do in fact result in their desires?

What is the secret? Routines or Habits! Habits are repeated patterns of behavior. If the repeated pattern of behavior is a good one, the right one, what you have is a repeated cycle of achievements and merits. It is as simple as that. As Frank Hall Crane put it, "Habits are (even) safer than rules; you don't have to watch them. And you don't have to keep them either. They keep you." In any case, once you establish a good set of habits, everything else falls in line for you.

In this chapter, I am bent on convincing you on why you need good and productive habits, and I shall waste no time further.

## Be Able to Persevere Better

Nothing good comes easily. "Life is full of ups and downs" as they say. But do you know that in every up, there are other ups and downs, and it is the same for every down? The point I am trying to make is that life is an intricate layer of complexities and unpredictability. A good business plan can be impeded by a panic in the financial market. But if you have made a habit of reviewing your previous steps, if you have made a habit of making sure all the prerequisites are checked before taking action, you won't find it difficult to persevere in difficult times. Why? Perseverance will have become second nature to you already.

## Build Healthier Working Relationships

Earlier, I demonstrated how bad habits could cost you relationships. The inverse is also true. Cultivating the right kind of habits puts you in the company of like persons. You will naturally repel people with negative habits and attract people of similar positive habits. Negative habits reduce your social grace and make conversations unproductive, discomfiting, and awkward for all parties involved. When you foster positive habits, it would be a joy to work and interact with you, leading to a better, harmonious relationship between you and your clients, employee, employers, and associates.

## Stand Out

Good habits allow you to stand out. When you stand out, it will only be a matter of time before you become outstanding. Yet, again, once you become outstanding, you are sure to become the standard, the one whose name is mentioned as a contrast when some others are being scolded. The recompense of good habits is a load of good thing and opportunities. If each time after a meeting at the school club or at the office, you get assigned tasks which you quickly complete and submit, you become the personification of efficiency. Anyone, except they have some other issues with you, will not be able to resist putting in a good word for you when an opportunity comes.

## Supercharge Your Way to Success

Good habits supercharge your way to success. What do I mean by this? With good habits, what is rather a steep road becomes a smooth plain. With good habits, what is a rather boring task becomes broken into chunks of smaller tasks you can easily complete in bits. With good habits, what is rather meant to discourage the weak-minded becomes a motivation for you to see something through. Good habits supercharge your way to success because they remove all forms of obstacles on your way to success, whether such obstacles are physical, financial, emotional or mental.

I shall not have written a complete book for you if I do not make recommendations on habits that can achieve everything I have discussed in this chapter and earlier in this book. In the next chapter, I shall discuss some important habits for you to form and why they are important.

# CHAPTER 8
# POSITIVE HABITS YOU SHOULD IMBIBE

*"Successful people aren't born that way. They become successful by establishing the habit of doing things unsuccessful people don't like to do."*

—William Makepeace Thackeray

We are creatures of habits; by habits, we fall, and by habits, we rise. Why then not strive to develop those habits that will only lead to our uplift rather than our fall in life? To help achieve success in life, I have earlier shown you why you should avoid bad habits, and I have even discussed some of the really ugly ones you need to avoid as well as their effects on your life. Here are some of the positive ones you should look to make a fixture of your routine.

## Wake up Early

If those who have really achieved greatness in life slept for much of their time, they would not have become the people we know them to be today. While you may not have to stay awake in the night crunching lines of codes as Bill Gates did, you also do not have to spend more of your time in bed. Do not be slothful. Get enough good sleep; make a habit of a good sleep pattern, but that pattern should have you waking up early. The early hours of the morning are the most productive hours mentally. When you wake up early too, you get to plan your day out and set the ball rolling before half of the world knows it's a new day already. That you get to work or school early is just an added bonus.

## Meditate

Meditation does not require you to subscribe to a belief system. It is just a system of deep reflection that can be used to achieve relaxation and peace of mind. You need your mind to be in the right state for the day's grind, and how better can you put your mental parts together than by meditation? There are many techniques out there, and you only need to get a book or read articles online about them. Meditation can be done in the morning, at work, or even after work in the evening. Meditation is one habit you will find in almost every great personality's life. It is that important.

## Exercising

Health is wealth, they say, and you must seek to keep yourself in the best possible state of health. You can prevent sickness and stay in good shape physically and mentally by exercising regularly. Make a habit of exercising every morning (just twenty pushups or sit-ups can go a long way to set things right in the physical, biochemical factory we call the human body). If you make a habit of waking up early, you will have enough time to meditate and exercise. If you do not have enough time to exercise sufficiently in the mornings, you can always do it in the evening. You should just find a way to work it into your day.

## Eating Healthy

You need to be careful with what you put into your body whether in the form of food, drink, and even drugs. Eating healthy is a must for good health. Food provides you with the right kind of nutrients you need for your work but only if you eat it in the right quantities and proportions. Eat right and live right; that is the code. Together with exercise, eating right will help you stay fitter and fresher for longer to deliver success.

## Read and Write

Reading makes a fine mind, writing an even better mind. These two acts help you grow intellectually. Through reading, you gain ideas that you never knew existed. It could even be an idea you know that is being shown in a new light. Reading increases your knowledgebase. But do you know what writing does? It gives clarity to your thoughts. It doesn't matter what you are writing; just put pen to paper every day. Put down your goals, aims, and plans; it gives them concrete form, and they take on a life of themselves when you put them down. You do not even need to be a superstar writer to put down the things in your mind for your own consumption. Write to yourself every day even if you do not intend to share with anyone. Reading and writing never harmed anyone. Rather, they could become your best tools for self-development.

## Set Goals

After making a habit of all the previously-mentioned activities, then, you need to learn to set goals. Too many people blunder through life with only a faint idea of what they want from it. Many are on a journey towards a vague destination. It's no wonder then that many end up arriving nowhere. You do not need to join this ill-fated trip. Rather, you are already in the ideal state of mind and physical health to be able to decide what direction you want to go in life. You should probably have read books on how to set goals and what goals to set. If you have not yet, I should tell you the first and most important rule of goal setting which is essentialism. This means you should not bite off more than you can chew. Determine the next right thing, and focus on it. Give it your all and move to the next thing on your plan. When you have achieved that thing, start the process all over for a new goal.

## Perseverance

This a very good habit that helps one sail through life smoothly. Life is never a bed of roses. The ups and downs that seem to pop each time one turns the corner seem insurmountable. However, with constant perseverance, you will be able to pass each difficult stage in life, mentally unscathed so that you have enough energy to move on in life with other endeavors. Perseverance is a mental habit rather than physical, but that does not render it any less important.

## Positive Thinking

Nothing frustrates your efforts more than negativity. If you are not positive about your ability to get something done, you will do a shoddy job to validate your doubts. Negativity shows there is not enough enthusiasm to achieve something great. Make a habit of positive thinking, and you will stop seeing obstacles but already crossed hurdles. You can practice positive affirmations to boost your positive thinking.

## Develop Money Management Skills

If you have a bad money-saving habit, you will never have enough for yourself. Perhaps a lesson can be learned in the story of Vanderbilt, the great American philanthropist and 11th-century millionaire. While working the sailing boats in America, Vanderbilt saved a lot until he got a better job on a ship and still saved a lot. In fact, he eventually bought that very ship and ended up owing a fleet. How did he achieve this? He made a habit of money management. He never spent impulsively and never fell for the constant invitation to acquire things just for the fun of it. Make a habit of monitoring your finances, and you will realize you are richer than you had earlier imagined.

## Cultivate Social Skills

You cannot be an island unto yourself. You are human, and you exist in a human society. Whether you like it or not, you will have to relate with others. Why not do that in the best way it can be done? Cultivate good social skills online and offline. Learn to converse with people with pure and sincere intent. Smile at people, and they will smile back at you. Appear clean and neat always. Your appearance is your cover letter and calling card. Cultivate social grace and eliminate awkwardness. You will be thankful you did.

# CONCLUSION

It was the famous Greek philosopher, Aristotle who said, "We are what we repeatedly do..." and that singular truth has held firm and true for a whole millennium. Our habits define us, and what we can/cannot do. They can aid or impede our desire to be successful and happy. We are our habits, and our habits are us.

Nobody ever got to the top with toxic habits pervading his life. It is impossible to have unhealthy habits and stay disease-free for too long. When you keep negative habits, you breed an aura of negativity around you. You keep your own abilities at a minimal level and allow unneeded distractions. It's like weighing yourself down unnecessarily, and you simply cannot get going with these habits holding you down.

If, however, you commit to uprooting the negative habits and replacing them with more positive habits, you can drive around life on a turbocharged engine. There is absolutely no door that positive habits cannot open, no obstacle it cannot get you around. It has been the secret that the truly great personalities in history have employed. They learned the power of habit early and held fast onto it. They knew all they had to do was sit down and pick out the negative habits that were at loggerheads with what they wanted from life. Then, they replace them with more positive ones.

You have that choice today too. The ball is in your court right now. Are you going to sit down and watch it bounce around as negative habits ensure you achieve absolutely nothing worthwhile in life? Or are you going to act like successful people by taking charge and striking negative habits out of your life today, and create for yourself the atomic habits that can assure you of success? The choice is yours!!!

Thank you for reading this book. I am quite sure you have gotten new ideas and fresh knowledge for building the right catalog of habits. If you would like to:

- Overcome Self-doubt,
- End voluntary social isolation,
- Learn how to build great communication skills,
- Improve your career prospects,
- Build your happiness project and,
- Enjoy more fruitful associations and relationship with other people,

...then, I recommend that you read the book, *"Introvert Power: Achieve Happiness in Life by Applying Simple Success Principles for Introverts"* by me, available on the Amazon KDP store. It is a great, enlightening read that can help you build on the foundation this book lays for happiness and success.

Made in the USA
Middletown, DE
10 July 2020